7 Rs of Leadership and Life

A. Valletta

Copyright © 2023 A. Valletta
All rights reserved
First Edition

NEWMAN SPRINGS PUBLISHING
320 Broad Street
Red Bank, NJ 07701

First originally published by Newman
Springs Publishing 2023

ISBN 979-8-89061-042-3 (Paperback)
ISBN 979-8-89061-043-0 (Digital)

Printed in the United States of America

To our family and support system: Mom (Toni) and Pop (John) Policarpo, Mom-Mom Mary, Poppy-Lou, and Brother-Lou Valletta.

Introduction

Sometimes in the fast-paced, technological world that we live in, we lose some of the characteristics that are central to being a member of a community: empathy, relationships, and love. Being a part of a community depends on everyday human interaction. Gone are the days of bank tellers knowing the name of every patron; we have mobile banking for that. Gone are the days of greeting your fellow passengers on the bus; we have headphones in anyway. So how can we thrive in this ever-changing world while retaining our core characteristics of maintaining our position in our community?

Every day for one month, *from Sunday to Sunday*, together we will review an R, a characteristic, a verb, to practice in our everyday lives. This process, woven into your daily life, will build positive habits, effective leadership, and genuine and meaningful human interaction.

As my children grew into their adolescent years, especially my maturing son, who was the inspiration of the *7 Rs of Leadership and Life*, we began discussing some basics of human interaction and guidelines of life. Through these conversations, the first seven of our Rs of leadership and life were born. Our foundation for this method will start with the seven Rs that will serve as our framework, our week 1. I start with respect, and we move to responsibility, resolve, right thing, readiness, recreation, and relationship. This framework of week 1 will become a framework for the rest of our month together.

Days 1–7

Day 1—Respect

Every interaction that we have—with family, friends, nature, and the world—should have respect as the foundation. Our intentions should always be to understand the wants and needs of each person or structure with which we are interacting.

There are certain rules of living in a society that are adhered to by respectful members of a community. Speaking loudly on your cell phone in a restaurant, for example, is deemed rude and disrespectful. This behavior shows a lack of respect for fellow patrons in the restaurant, employees of the restaurant, dining companions, and yourself.

Sometimes, respect is viewed on a more global scale. We know that it is disrespectful to our neighbors and community if we litter. It is unsightly and rude. Littering is also disrespectful to our planet; littering causes harm and can kill our wildlife and plant life.

These may seem like obvious examples, but we see these societal rules being broken day in and day out.

We all have busy lives. We all want things done quickly and efficiently. What kind of behavior do you use when tasks are not completed quickly and efficiently? We are all sometimes guilty of "exploding"—myself included. However, when you are a bystander watching these types of interactions, it becomes clear that being testy with an employee at an establishment is inappropriate.

I recently was next in line at a very popular bakery down the shore—or at the beach as you may say. The customer at the counter asked for round rolls. The flustered employee accidentally handed the woman long rolls. A scene of hysterics and yelling ensued, while tears filled the employee's eyes. I approached the counter, asked for what I wanted, and I was also given the wrong kind of roll. I let the associate know, and all she could do was apologize and shake her head. I smiled at her, gave her $20, and let her know that not every customer will be disrespectful for a silly and trivial mistake. Her entire demeanor changed, and I hope her day was turned around.

Disrespecting someone does not help them fix their mistakes any faster; in fact, it is counterproductive. Mistakes happen, and it is our job as members of a community to encounter each obstacle with respect and understanding.

It is imperative that we implement this overarching premise of respect in our workplace. Each encounter that one has must be one of respect and honor. I have had my fair share of jobs in the past. I have led teams of ten, and I have led full organizations. In each role in which I serve, I guide and coach; I never demand nor dictate. This is the result of respecting the people on my teams and trusting in their skill sets.

Whenever I start a new role with an organization, I speak with each individual within the first thirty days. At the very start of each of these meetings, I let each person know that I work for them. They do not work for me; they work for the clients, partners, and customers. If I deliver the tools they need for their success, I respect their expertise to succeed. This framework sets up a baseline culture of mutual respect and lets every employee know that we are on a level playing field—playing for the accomplishments and prosperity of the same team.

We should always give others our respect. That speaks to our character and our human nature. Further, we must always remember that we gain respect when we give that respect genuinely and honestly.

How could you put these ideas into practice in your personal, professional, and social lives—today, tomorrow, and for the rest of your life? How will you respect the drive-through worker who messed up your order? How will you respect your coworker who hasn't recently been meeting productivity goals?

Day 2—Responsibility

Yesterday, we discussed that all of our interactions must be respectful. Today, we discuss responsibility. In every encounter with others, we have to ensure we are accepting responsibility. This goes far beyond taking credit for things that go well and taking blame for things that go poorly. Both of those are key to taking responsibility, but we must dive deeper. Every one of our interactions, every one of our daily tasks, and every one of our actions must be handled to the very best of our ability—that is acting with responsibility and having integrity.

When we drive, for example, it is crucial that we do that to the best of our abilities. Being negligent in this case could be life-threatening. We are responsible when we fasten our seatbelts, use our turn signals, and when we obey the speed limit signs. We all know the slogan "Drink responsibly." We hear that after every alcohol commercial on TV. How can we implement that? By appointing a designated driver on a night out on the town—or using a rideshare service.

Just as in driving, we must be responsible in our business interactions as well. I implemented a method called CARES while running the IT department at a financial institution. CARES is an acronym that stands for courteous, accurate, responsible, and empathic service. This acronym served as a reminder that I CARE for my team, and their mission was to CARE for the customers, clients, and coworkers. This was a quick and easy reminder to ensure that each interaction was met with this idea of "acting responsibly" that we are discussing today.

I then changed the name of our IT Helpdesk to IT CARES. This shift in mindset from the team shifted our client experiences. We became responsible for providing the best IT services possible so that our customers, our bankers, could have the best possible experience. We also implemented a CARES survey card that our technicians left with our service partners after every service call. Satisfaction skyrocketed—for every one missed opportunity, we had fifty positive comments. This CARES model made me responsible for my team and made my team responsible for CARE-ing for our clients.

Taking just the responsibility aspect of CARES, as that is our mission for today, how can you practice this in your life? How will you act responsibly in your personal and professional lives? I challenge you to have integrity in all of your tasks today—from closing a business deal, to driving home from work, to picking up that ice cube instead of kicking it under the refrigerator.

Day 3—Resolve

There are few things in our lives over which we have 100 percent control. We can take our difficulties and let them control us, or we can use them to strengthen our resolve. Our goal today is to be in tune with, and have control over, our outward emotions and mannerisms. It certainly is much easier to lash out than be even-keeled about circumstances. It can be referred to as a Zen mindset, an inner peace, or serenity. It all boils down to the Golden Rule that we all learned in elementary school: treat others the way you want to be treated. I have failed with 100 percent resolve every day of my life. It is a continued practice, which is why I strive to work on strengthening my resolve—so I can be a better son, husband, father, CEO, coworker, or board member, so I can be a better person.

In the earlier parts of my career, I was known for letting people "have it." Losing my temper with business partners that delivered services to my firm was a regular occurrence for me. While I was always fair with my expectations of partners, I did not always go about resolving the problem well or correctly. The story would go something like this: the service was not delivered up to par, I'd get on the phone and lash out, they'd apologize (and secretly curse me in their heads), and a resolution would happen.

Fast forward a month, and the problems would occur again. I needed to change the way I approached these scenarios because this is not practical for business, and I didn't like who I was in those instances of losing my temper. Today, I ask probing questions about the challenges, listen to the responses I receive, and use influence (not emotion) to ensure an outcome that everyone is happy with.

Our entire life is not spent in the office, though, nor should it be. So strengthening our resolve in our personal lives is even more crucial. Does it feel good to get around a car that cut me off to "show them"? Of course. Is it easier to place blame and lash out than to think about root causes with family? Sometimes! But that doesn't make for a happy (or safe, in the circumstance of the car) life.

Many years ago, I received a phone call from my son's friend. We were all on vacation together, enjoying a relaxing week at the beach. The boys had all gone out to the boardwalk, and the rest of us stayed back to watch a movie and get into bed early. My son knew the rules—wake me up when you get home. This time, I was woken up before he returned home. The phone rang, and I was greeted with a, "Mr. V., can you come pick us up?"

I hopped in the car, fuming that these boys were not only drinking, but they weren't even careful enough to ensure safe travel back home. I practiced my speech in the car. When I pulled up, the boys skulked in with their heads hung low, and I tempered my rehearsed lecture and simply said, "You did the right thing by calling me."

Their safety was far more important than that lecture (which they did receive the next day). If I would've screamed at them like I wanted to, they would have regretted calling me and, even worse, not chosen to do so if there was a next time. Acting with resolve in this circumstance was a life lesson for those boys and a potentially lifesaving one that they will remember forever.

Today, our goal and challenge is to act with resolve. Next time you are in an infuriating situation, take a deep breath, try to give the benefit of the doubt, and show your family and coworkers that you love and respect them by your actions.

Day 4—Right Thing

Doing the right thing should be easy, right? We are told from the time we are children to do the right thing by playing and sharing with everyone, inviting the whole sixth-grade class to the birthday party, inviting the kid sitting alone to your lunch table in high school, and the list goes on. But do we always do the right thing? Of course not; it is part of our human nature to falter and make mistakes.

I asked a group of people once to think about the ten worst things they've ever done in their lives. Afterward, I asked each person if they knew at the time of the action if what they were doing was wrong. With remorseful looks on their faces, they all said yes. It is instilled in us from birth what the right thing is versus the wrong thing, so why do we sometimes do the wrong thing anyway?

When you take your dog for a walk, and he "goes," you know the right thing to do is to pick it up. But what if you are in a rush? The ten seconds it takes to scoop is all the time it takes to go from doing the wrong thing to doing the right thing.

Another scenario—what if you need to borrow your wife's car because yours is in the shop? You're rushing from work to get home because you're hungry. You're almost home, and the fuel light turns on; she's almost out of gas. Do you return home to eat? Or do you go to the gas station to fill it up so she doesn't have to later tonight as she rushes off to her night shift? Doing the right thing in our personal lives makes us better people, and it will also improve our relationships.

Throughout college, my daughter complained about group projects. She was doing most of the work, and her group mates would all get the A that she did, but they maybe did 10 percent of the work. Although I wanted to soothe her anger, I knew that it may not get better as she navigated through school into the professional world.

My daughter's story of this one particularly lazy group with which she was teamed sparked my memory of a middle manager with whom I worked. This middle manager, let's call him Tim, was boasting in a keynote speech he was delivering about an idea that he had for developing and implementing a new program. It was brought to my attention that Tim was taking credit for an idea that was not his.

In this instance, the right thing for me to do as a leader was to approach Tim about the situation. Through our discussion and my questioning, Tim confessed to deceiving his audience during his keynote. We discussed ways to make this right. In the end, Tim came clean about his misleading speech in a full team staff meeting. From there, we worked on rehabilitating the broken trust that Tim had created. Tim learned, through that challenge, a valuable lesson on doing the right thing, and he went on to be a direct report, a wonderful leader, and a great teammate.

What is a right thing that you have been putting off lately? Do you need to apologize to a coworker? Did you tell your spouse you'd clean the garage but you keep promising "tomorrow"? Whatever it is, our challenge today is to step up and do one right thing.

Day 5—Readiness

Readiness is a function of discipline and focus. I cannot count the number of times a soccer coach or dance teacher instilled in my children the idea that "if you arrive on time, you are late." If you walk through the door at 10:59, and practice starts at 11:00, how will you change your clothes and shoes, warm up, stretch, and be in the ready position all in one minute? It is impossible. By arriving just fifteen to thirty minutes early, you set yourself up for success, not only physically, but mentally as well.

If my son was stressed about arriving at a soccer game on time, there wouldn't be any way for him to prepare mentally to stop soccer balls from entering his net. This exercise of arriving early eventually becomes a habit, and that habit helps us have better focus and better readiness throughout our lives. To this day, my daughter will arrive at work thirty minutes early. Fifteen of those minutes are for her to have a "car sit," to help her mentally prepare to enter the building. The second half of that time is going into the building and setting up all of the supplies she needs for the day.

I recently watched a documentary about the late and great Kobe Bryant. No one would argue that Kobe was one of the best basketball players of all time. How did he get there? Throughout the documentary, it was evident that he demanded nothing short of excellence from himself and his teammates. He propelled everyone forward to better themselves, which in turn made him even better. He was continually honing his skills—working out both physically and mentally to prepare himself for games. His regime included intense physical workouts that could only be done by a top athlete, and his diet was also impeccable. His entire routine prepared him, and he was continually striving for readiness in his craft. He even stated that none of his teammates could outwork him.

That dedication helped Kobe Bryant to be ready in every aspect of the game. There is no doubt that Kobe was always a step above his peers. I think it is a safe assumption that a lot of that has to do with his commitment to readiness. My daughter has a funny saying that she always uses that she got from pop culture: "Stay ready so you don't have to get ready."

Why is readiness important in business? If we are always preparing ourselves and setting ourselves up for success, we will always be as ready as we can be! Sometimes, it is as simple as being proactive to prevent being reactive. If you keep a planner with all of your meeting times, you will know when you are busy and when you are not. This way, you will never have to "react" by canceling a meeting because you double-booked yourself.

What is one way that you can be proactive today? Is it setting up that meeting with your team so you can work out problems in a project? Is it diffusing tension with a coworker so it doesn't escalate? Find just one thing that you can do so that you are "ready" for something bigger.

Day 6—Recreation

Recreation is important for all of us, beginning at birth. As a child, it may consist of playing basketball with friends, joining the church choir, or having playdates with your cousins. For this, recreation, I believe, is the most flexible of the Rs. This particular R boils down to 3 Fs: faith, family/friends, and fun!

Let's start with faith. To have faith in ourselves, our world, humanity, and a higher power (if you believe) is paramount to our happiness. Faith helps us hold onto hope. Faith helps us to have a positive attitude that we will have blessings and abundance in our lives. It helps us be confident in ourselves and our surroundings. People often ask why I am not a gambling man. You cannot find me betting on Sunday night football, nor can you find me sitting at a card table in Atlantic City. Why?

There is no need for me to bet on outside events because I bet on myself. When you bet on yourself and you practice being the best you (by keeping the Rs at the forefront of your mind), you always win. Knowing that I am the best me I can be, I will always have a positive outcome; even a mistake is a lesson learned in my eyes. Having this amount of faith in myself helps me to have abundant gratitude for all of the blessings bestowed upon me. How do you bet on yourself? What makes you have faith in yourself for who you are and all that you will achieve?

We start our lives with family and friends. We are born into a family, and we create a network of friends throughout our lives. Having this support system is vital to our success, and being part of the support system for those we love is vital to our purpose and happiness. It is often said that to feel love, we must love. How do you work on love? How do you practice loving others and yourself every day?

Love is a feeling, but it is so much more than that. Love cannot be passive. To be active in the love that we pour into our community, we need to work at it. Here is a great visual of LOVE by Robert Indiana. If you look at the visual, you will see that the O is askew. The O is said to be askew because love is never perfect, and it is something to work on every day.

We can absolutely work at love by being respect-ful and responsible, by living with resolve, by doing the right thing, by building relationships, and by being ready.

Finally, *fun*! We must leave time for ourselves to enjoy this life that we have worked so hard to build. My children often make fun of me: the CEO, the leader, the suit-wearing, cufflink-donning, serious man, busting out into dance moves in the candy aisle of Five Below. Or for sitting in a parking lot, blasting pop music and singing along after going out to a fancy dinner.

Do I do it to make them laugh? Maybe. But I always tell them, "I am serious all day long. I have to make decisions twelve hours out of the day. I just want to have some *fun*!" So after your long day, whether you are an intern grabbing the fourth coffee for your boss, or you are that intern's boss, don't forget to bust out a move if that's what makes you happy!

Weaving this tapestry of faith, community, and fun through the R of recreation leads us to a fulfilled life. We are able to see, appreciate, and enjoy our many blessings.

Day 7—Relationship

Building relationships is all about connecting, which is something I love to do. In life and in business, building relationships is crucial, and these relationships should be built on trust and integrity. Just like love, we must work at building trust every single day.

Relationships within a family and within a group of friends are as unique as the people in the relationships. I can't tell you how to build those relationships. But in business? That is a different challenge. In every business relationship, we must delicately communicate, connect, discuss, negotiate, influence, compromise, and develop win-win dealings. If we fail, or we are perceived to have failed, at any one of these skills, our business relationships can suffer—or end.

As an example, instead of a relationship builder, I'd like to focus on a relationship breaker. A gentleman worked for me; let's call him Blake. Blake was as skilled an engineer as any boss would want. He knew hardware, and he knew software; he could do it all. A truly rare combination of gifts.

But Blake had a habit of letting everyone on the team know that they were not as smart as he was. If someone on the team had a problem and approached him, he would let them know that they were stupid for needing help. If someone went about something in a different way than he would, he made sure to talk down to them. I had numerous talks with him, sent him to training, and explained that he needed to take the time to rebuild the relationships that he had broken.

After six months of this repeating unacceptable pattern of behavior (even with my attempted interventions), I gave him forty-five days to seriously correct his behavior, or he'd need to find another place of employment. On paper, this guy had it all, and he knew more than most. But business is not a solo sport. It was ultimately my responsibility to ensure that everyone on my team had a professional environment in which they could thrive, and someone breaking the relationships within the team is not something that any business can afford.

In your own relationships, how do you thrive? How can you be better? Take a look at the Rs. Are you genuinely checking all of the boxes? Are you respectful and responsible? Do you have resolve and take the high road? Do you try to do the right thing? Do you approach situations prepared and ready? Take these actions into your relationships and watch them flourish.

Day 8–14

Day 8—Raise for Responsibility

Now that we have hit the 7 big Rs in week 1, I want to focus on some finer points in this next week of Rs. Raise is where my mind initially went. I thought of how we raise people up in our daily lives. Sometimes, it is praising others; sometimes, it is doing a good deed for a stranger or giving back to the community.

We have a convenience store in the Northeast called Wawa. Now, us Northeasterners are not necessarily known for our patience or kindness, but Wawa has different rules. A person will wait ten to fifteen seconds just to hold the door for you. Everyone knows of this unwritten rule, and it is such a nice way to raise someone up, especially in the hustle and bustle of daily life.

We also need to raise others up in our work environments. It is everyone's job to create this type of culture in our office spaces. How can you bring these small gestures into your workspace? I have a phrase that I often like to say: "I work for the team, and the team works for the clients." I like to model raising up to my team members, and by so doing, the culture is there so they more naturally do the same for our clients.

This comes from small gestures, like ensuring the coffee creamer in the refrigerator is stocked, and through larger gestures, like publicly acknowledging a win by a team member. If we all try to perform gestures like this, even just once a day, the dynamic and culture of our environments can shift dramatically.

Day 9—Rally for Relationships

When we think of a rally, the word *pep* usually precedes it, like a high school pep rally for the football team's big homecoming game. Even though that's where the mind tends to immediately jump, we also rally for our families. Imagine: you just worked an eighty-hour week, and it is Sunday, and your daughter has a dance recital. All you want to do is sleep in. But what do you do? You rally! You sit in the front row of the theater with a smile on your face and a bouquet of flowers in your hands. Or a loved one is terminally ill, and a to-do list of a few dozen items lands on your spouse's shoulders. What do you do? You rally, you comfort, you help. It is natural and necessary if we are to have successful personal relationships.

Now let's think about the workplace. When a problem arises, and a solution seems impossible, what do you do? Cast blame? Push it onto someone else? As we addressed in week 1, our relationships are so vital and oftentimes delicate that we cannot do this. Instead, we need to have a pep rally! Maybe not with cheerleaders and football players. But a rally, nonetheless.

Rally up the office and bring in the problem-solvers—discuss, design, develop, deploy, and debrief. Come together to discuss the issue, design a plan of attack, develop your ideas further, deploy the plan, and debrief after all is complete. When we rally like this, our relationships strengthen, and the product that we are creating together improves.

Day 10—Ramp Up for Readiness

As we discussed in week 1, readiness is key to success. But how do we prepare so that we are always ready? Let's think about exiting a suburban town to drive into the city, and you take the highway. Do you go from 20 mph on the residential streets to 65 mph on the four-lane highway? Of course, not! In fact, you have an acceleration ramp to get you prepared for the high speeds ahead.

How do you ramp yourself up for a busy day of meetings? I like to meditate for twenty minutes and have a cup of coffee in the morning. It helps ground me for the day ahead. Ramping up often means a routine, a ritual, a warmup for the day/tasks ahead.

If you do not have one already, think of a small ritual that you can integrate into your life to ramp yourself up for readiness and success each day. It is easy to hit snooze, to scroll social media for twenty minutes under the covers, or to run out the door without making your bed. But does this ramp you up for readiness, or does it create chaos at the start of your day?

Day 11—Rapid for Respect

In life and business, it is essential that we get things done and get them done quickly. This is where this "R" comes from—"rapid" solutions for respect. We do not want to do things so rapidly that we cut corners or bulldoze the people around us, but we also need to be quick with our responses to respect everyone's time. Think about being in line at a grocery store the day before Thanksgiving. Do you want your cashier to take twenty minutes per person, carefully wrapping each vegetable? No. But do you want them throwing your canned cranberry sauce into your cart like a quarterback? Also no. There is a sweet spot of urgency and care.

I had a rapid response team when working for a large financial services company. This team was deployed when complex issues arose in the banking systems we had in place. While the impetus of the service was to be rapid in managing the problems—

and we were—we ran into problems in other areas. Our clients often felt frustrated because our communication was lacking. We wanted to *go, go, go*; but our clients needed reassurance that things were being resolved, and they wanted to know how. We needed to hit that delicate balance of restoring to normal quickly but also having customer service skills. How do you hit that "sweet spot" of rapid service for respect in your life?

Day 12—Radiance for Recreation

Radiance for recreation means approaching our interactions within our family relationships and friendships with lightness and brightness in our hearts. For example, I see a lot of posts on social media that have thirty-plus comments beneath them that include mean comments, people bickering back and forth, and people just being flat-out rude to one another.

These types of interactions are needless, and the individuals posting them are not exhibiting class or radiance. Disagreements happen, but do you really need to be disrespectful in the comment section of your second cousin's selfie because you don't agree with what she said at Thanksgiving last year?

Radiance can also be brought into your private thoughts as well. Are you receiving the blessings in your life with brightness in your heart? Hopefully, you approach your promotion, your new house, and your spouse with radiance—because those are blessings. But blessings are easier to approach with radiance than the things that we perceive to be inconvenient. If you spill your coffee on your favorite button-down and have to turn back to change clothes, how can you approach that with radiance?

I once read a blog post about a man who had to drive his daughter to school because she missed the bus, and it made him late for a meeting. That is an inconvenience, right? But the blog post goes on to explain that being late caused this man to miss being in New York's Twin Towers on 9/11/2001 at 8:46 a.m. This was a blessing in disguise for this man. The blog post contained about a dozen stories similar to that one.

So maybe next time you spill your coffee, or your teenager misses the bus, or you need to stop at a convenience store because you forgot to set up the coffee pot the night before, think about how that could be a blessing in disguise, and approach the situation with radiance.

Day 13—Responsive for the Right Thing

One of the keys to effective communication is ensuring that we are responding to situations the right way. If one of your team members comes to you and informs you that there has been a mess up on a project, there are two ways to respond to this. First, you can get worked up and start being angry, rude, and demeaning to the individual. The second way to respond to this is to take a deep breath, ask questions, and facilitate a solution as a team leader.

This second response is the obvious "right thing" response, but it is not always the easiest. Just keep in mind, your team is full of people who know how to do their jobs, they try their best, and they want the projects and the team to succeed.

Any dilemmas that may happen are part of life. Instead of getting your blood pressure up about a snafu, try to take a step back and evaluate how you can best serve your team here and now. Respond in the right way. Maybe the "right thing" is to extend the deadline. Maybe the "right thing" is to oversee the project from now on. Or maybe the "right thing" is to simply encourage your team that they know what the best course of action is and to try again. How can you respond in the right way today?

Day 14—Resilient for Resolve

Being resilient is important to keep the momentum of your life moving forward. If you are not resilient, a "no" from a job interview can set you back instead of propelling you forward.

How can you practice being resilient in your life? When I am faced with a less-than-ideal circumstance, I say a quick prayer that I have been saying my whole life. I know other individuals who recite an inspirational quote to themselves or revisit an old poem that brings them comfort.

My daughter told me about a new trend that is becoming increasingly popular among her colleagues as well. A person says an affirming phrase to themselves while looking in the mirror—an affirmation. Some of the examples can be as simple as "I am strong, I am worthy, I am smart," or they can be more involved and specific to the types of obstacles the individual is facing.

How do you arm yourself to be resilient against the obstacles you face? Taking a few seconds to do this will help you to be in control if you can be or to manage the situation if you cannot control it.

Day 15–21

Day 15—Remedy for Resolve

How can we fix the things in our lives to help us have resolve in all situations? How can we create a prescription—a remedy—to help us succeed in having resolve as our baseline? Our resilience R from yesterday and this R of today are quite similar. Our practice of resilience is something we can implement at the moment to keep pushing us in the right direction.

This "remedy" is a prescription you take daily—something that will keep you in a great mindset more often than not. My remedy is meditation. I meditate twice a day to put myself in the mindset to tackle many situations in my daily life.

I first went to a transcendental meditation class with my wife. We both needed an outlet to help us handle some of the stressors in our lives. Adding time into my daily life for this remedied some of the behavior struggles I was facing. Where I lacked patience before, I am finding myself to be more patient.

Find a place in your life that needs a remedy. What is a prescription you can take for yourself to heal? If you lack confidence, maybe those aforementioned—positive affirmations—can be your daily habit. If you lack patience, maybe try meditating like me. Whatever it is, this remedy should have positivity and should position your mindset to be the best that you can be in your daily life, both personal and business.

Day 16—Reliable for Recreation

Reliability is a skill in our everyday lives, and it is necessary. Do you show up to work Monday through Friday on time? Do you ensure that there is enough dog food in the cabinet for the week? These are ways to be reliable. These "grown-up" tasks require reliability so that you maintain your job and your family structure functions without unnecessary hiccups.

What about in your recreation? Are you reliable in that branch of your life? Say you promised your son you'd go to his soccer game on Friday night, but you had a horrible day at work. You can choose to bail on him, or you can choose to be reliable for him and show up. Not only is this family time paramount to our happy family structure and life balance, it is also a lesson to your children to honor their commitments.

Or say you promised your neighbor you'd help him close his pool for the winter, but you just really don't feel like it when Saturday morning at 8:00 a.m. rolls around. When we let the nonessential tasks of our lives slip, we are not enjoying our lives, nor are we there for the people that we love. What is one way you can be more reliable in your personal life this week?

Day 17—Receptive for Respect

We have all heard the phrase "give respect to get respect." But how is it exactly that we can respect someone? One way is to be receptive. When your child comes to you crying because she broke her favorite toy, you hug her and tell her something comforting. And when a colleague is having a bad day because his cat has died, you could offer to pick up his slack and let him have an early day.

But what about when it is something that you don't understand or agree with? What if it is a stranger who needs help finding a quiet area because it is prayer time in his religion? Or what if a coffee shop employee is sporting a pin representing a political belief opposite to your own? We live in an ever-changing climate. And if you are reading this from the USA, we have just about every religion/nonbelief, lifestyle, culture, sexual orientation, race, and political viewpoint on the planet. That's why we are called a melting pot, after all!

If someone is living their life differently from how you live your own, be receptive, be respectful, and be curious. When we approach everyone with the intent to understand rather than to judge, we can have very positive learning opportunities.

Day 18—Recognition for Responsibility

When we are recognized for the great work we have done, it feels good. It is our responsibility to our colleagues and to our families and peers to recognize them as well. When your Facebook friend posts about the birth of their new grandchild, we have many options. We can scroll past, we can hit the Like button, or we can leave a beautiful congratulatory message in their comments. Better yet, we can give them a call!

This same mindset can shift into our professional lives. A great leader will take the time to recognize their employees for meeting goals. This can be as big as landing a new client or as small as getting a file completed early. No accomplishment is too small to recognize! I suggest that leaders give their praise and recognition publicly. This not only makes the achiever feel proud, it also creates a tone of cooperation in the office.

On the opposite side of this, I like to suggest any "reprimanding" be done privately. While accomplishments are meant to be shared, if you need to address someone for something less than satisfactory, this should always be done in private. This not only protects people from feeling embarrassed, it will also retain their dignity and keep morale high.

What can you do today to publicly recognize someone on your team?

Day 19—Refresh for Readiness

We have learned the importance of being ready; if we are always prepared, we are always "on." For our productivity, this is great. But what about our mental health? Just like a computer, we often need a refresh.

I have personally found that "shutting down" for at least ten business days is extremely healthy in order to prevent burnout. It may feel like ten days is too long. However, have you ever taken a five-day vacation and didn't ever stop thinking about work? Our minds are still on. I suggest taking a full ten days to do something. This can be as extravagant as going on that trip to Italy that you always dreamed of, going to the lake upstate, or even as simple as a "staycation," where you sit on your front porch and take the time to actually taste your morning coffee.

Another way to refresh? Take a long four-day weekend for yourself. Sometimes those ten-day shut-downs are too far down the road. These small four-day weekends can serve as checkpoints for you to refresh yourself.

Plan out a time that would be good for you to take your refresh break, and act on it! We get that vacation time for a reason. You will come back from these breaks readier than ever!

Day 20—Remember
for Relationship

Do you know those commercials on TV about the husband scrambling because he forgot his wife's birthday? Those plots may get a cheap laugh, but no one enjoys feeling forgotten. Remembering is vital to our relationships.

Picking up the phone to call a friend on their birthday means so much. My father-in-law got a call from a former employee of his every single year on his birthday, without fail. All year long, he'd brag about how "Matt always calls me on my birthday." Being remembered means more to people than we realize. And we can perform these gestures all year long! It can be as simple as texting your friend because you found those hard-to-find cookies in the supermarket and you thought of him.

Whatever it is, make a conscious effort to reach out. I like to reach out to the majority of my contacts to wish those in my life a Happy New Year, Happy Fourth of July, or even just a Happy Friday! Think of five people you can reach out to today. They are only a text message away.

Day 21—Renew for the Right Thing

We talked about doing the right thing. Oftentimes, we need to renew our mindsets about what the "right thing" is. Check in with your goals, and renew your strategies to accomplish these goals.

A New Year's resolution is a good way people do this. Health, education, community service, and family relationship goals are always at the top of these types of lists. Let today be a checkpoint. Are you on your way there with your current habits? If not, make it a point to create a healthy foods grocery list, r finally take down the bag full of clothes to your nearest veterans association.

Day 22–28

Day 22—Rational for the Right Thing

Doing the right thing oftentimes means being rational. Being levelheaded is a hallmark of being a rational person. This is always easier said than done. However, taking one step back and two deep breaths can be the difference between hollering at someone on the sidewalk for blocking your way and gently saying, "Excuse me." I'm sure we can all think of a time when we let the heat of our anger influence us to make a poor decision. But let's make an effort today to take a step back and be more rational.

Day 23—Reasonable
for Recreation

My daughter nannied twins for a family, and when one of the boys would act out, their mom would always say, "You're being very unreasonable right now." As funny as that is to say to a toddler, it makes me really stop and think. What is a reasonable amount to expect of myself in my relationships, and what is a reasonable amount to expect of someone else?

If your spouse is a surgical resident in a hospital, it would probably be unreasonable to expect them home for dinner every night at 6:00 p.m. By the same token, I have busy hours, so it would be unreasonable for me to expect myself to watch every single Thursday night football game with my friends. Decide what is reasonable for you to expect yourself to do, and do it! We do not have to say yes to everything if it is outside of reasonable expectations. Give yourself the benefit of the doubt, and give others the same. Do all that you can today, but add "within reason" as a caveat.

Day 24—Rapport for Relationship

Building rapport with the people with whom we have relationships is essential to the health of those relationships. Understanding what your spouse needs from you is essential to a healthy marriage. Business relationships are the same way!

I build rapport with my teams by having "Ask Ang" sessions. Once a month, I bring in lunch for everyone, we sit down, and my team members can ask me anything they want—advice, family life, business deals, the list goes on! This is a great way to build rapport. My team knows who their leader is, and I get an understanding of what is important to the people in my office. How can you build a stronger connection with someone you work with today?

Day 25—Rare for Resolve

Rare things often have a lot of value. When there is a one-of-a-kind signed album from your favorite singer, you will probably be willing to pay far more for it than you would for a CD from the department store. On the same note, being a "rare" person, and as an employee, also gives you tremendous value. What traits make you unique and different for the better? Is it your precision, your kindness, your punctuality? Find what sets you apart from the crowd, and wear that proudly on your sleeve.

Day 26—Relentless for Responsibility

We often hear the phrase "Uh, he's relentless," and that usually means a bad thing. Your toddler may be relentless crying to get the last cookie. Your teenager may be relentless in arguing why she deserves the car this Friday night. But why can't relentlessness be a good thing? Why can't we be relentlessly patient? Or relentlessly kind? Why can't we be relentlessly responsible? Never wavering, never giving it up.

Be relentless in your preparation, your reliability, your respect. How can you take a simple task today and be relentlessly responsible with it? Maybe you can give your email extra proofreading before you send it to your boss. Maybe you can show up to the meeting five minutes early to help your admin set up the room. Whatever it is, go above and beyond in one thing today, and be relentless about it!

Day 27—Reassure for Respect

In our relationships, respect is necessary, but we also need to reassure people of our respect and that we are there for them judgment-free.

I once had a coworker / close friend who was arrested for embezzling funds. After this person came to me and took ownership of his mistakes, I was able to help him develop a plan for his legal issues and his future.

While this individual will never work in financial services again, he is able to provide for his family by working as a gig economy worker and helping his wife run her consulting business. He reassured me that this transgression was a once-in-a-lifetime mistake for which he atoned in the justice system, and I reassured him that I would help him get back on his feet. This type of reassurance helped our friendship grow.

Who can you reassure today? Maybe it is your teenager who you made stay home and study on a Friday night since he failed his quiz. Maybe you can tell him that once the math grade goes up, his freedoms will be reinstated. Or perhaps you can reassure a client that you hear her needs and that you will meet them like you always do. You will strengthen relationships and build even more trust this way.

Day 28—Retain for Readiness

In striving to be ready, our minds and bodies must retain all that we feed it. A person will undoubtedly do much better on an exam when they study for a week than when they study for a night. Why? More time preparing means more retaining!

To be ready, we need to give our minds the best possible chance for information retention! If you have an upcoming presentation, spend ten minutes per night the week before prepping, and you will do much better than if you spent one hour the night before. What can you start preparing for today that will give you the best chance of a positive future outcome?

Final Thoughts

My wife, Andrea, my daughter, Amanda, and I very much enjoyed capturing and sharing our seven Rs of leadership and life. We hope that you read one R per day and reread and implement the 7 Rs for the rest of your life. These 7 Rs are tried and true and have, in some way or fashion, been "lived" for many decades.

We mapped our 7 Rs with the well-known "System of the Sages of Sivana" and the "7 Habits of Highly Effective People." While we did not set out to mimic these two wonderful and powerful approaches, we learned that the similarities are significant.

We mapped the comparison in the chart and hope you find it useful.

7 Rs of Life and Leadership	"7 Virtues of Sivana" (Yogi Raman's mantra as outlined in the book *The Monk That Sold His Ferrari*)	7 Habits of Highly Effective People by Steven Covey
1. Respect	1. Mind	1. Begin with the End in Mind
2. Resolve	2. Self-Control	2. Seek First to Understand Then to be Understood
3. Responsibility	3. Purpose	3. Synergize
4. Readiness	4. Time Management	4. Be Proactive
5. Right-Thing	5. Self-Improvement	5. Put First Things First
6. Relationships	6. Helping Others	6. Think Win-Win
7. Recreation (Faith, Family, Friends, Fun, and Finances)	7. Living in the Moment	7. Sharpen the Saw

We also would like to leave one last thought. To be outstanding sometimes means focusing on the small stuff. So remember when living a better life or conducting yourself in business, the following action items do not require talent and map well to the 7 Rs. But they do require you to *want* to do better.

1. Being on time / being prepared = Readiness
2. Effort / work ethic = Responsibility
3. Body language = Resolve
4. Energy = Recreation
5. Attitude and passion = Relationships
6. Be coachable = Respect
7. Doing extra / going the extra mile = Right thing

About the Author

Angelo Valletta is currently President and CEO of Ben Franklin Technology Partners of Northeastern Pennsylvania, an early-stage technology investment firm. He worked in conjunction with his daughter, Amanda Valletta, who ghost wrote the book with assistance from his wife, Andrea Valletta. The inspiration for the book came from his son, Alex Valletta.

The family affair collaboration was not only enjoyable and fun but also drew them closer as a family and inspired them to live life with the *7 Rs* at the forefront of everything they do.

www.ingramcontent.com/pod-product-compliance
Lightning Source LLC
Chambersburg PA
CBHW031409160726
47993CB00003B/1157